The Second Realm: Book on Strategy

By: Smuggler and XYZ

LIBERTY UNDER ATTACK PUBLICATIONS

Copyleft Notice

⚑ LIBERTY UNDER ATTACK
ⒶPUBLICATIONS *tell your story*

Looking for your next read or listen?

1. **Adventures in Illinois Law: Witnessing Tyranny Firsthand** by Shane Radliff (Audiobook/Anthology)
2. **Adventures in Illinois Higher Education: Communist Indoctrination** by Shane Radliff (Audiobook/Anthology)
3. **An Illusive Phantom of Hope: A Critique of Reformism** by Kyle Rearden (Audiobook/Anthology)
4. **The Production of Security** by Gustave de Molinari (Audiobook)
5. **Are Cops Constitutional?** by Roger Roots (Audiobook)
6. **Vonu: The Search for Personal Freedom** by Rayo (Audiobook)
7. **Argumentation Ethics: An Anthology** by Hans-Herman Hoppe et al (Anthology)
8. **Just Below The Surface: A Guide to Security Culture** by Kyle Rearden (Audiobook/Anthology)
9. **Sedition, Subversion, and Sabotage, Field Manual No. 1: A Three Part Solution to the State** by Ben Stone (Audiobook)
10. **#agora** by anonymous (Paperback and Kindle)
11. **Vonu: A Strategy for Self-Liberation** by Shane Radliff (Paperback/Audiobook)
12. **Second Realm: Book on Strategy** by Smuggler and XYZ (Paperback)
13. **Vonu: The Search for Personal Freedom** by Rayo (Special Paperback Reprint/Audiobook)
14. **Vonu: The Search for Personal Freedom, Part 2 [Letters From Rayo]** (Paperback)
15. **Going Mobile** by Tom Marshall (Paperback/Audiobook)
16. **Anarchist to Abolitionist: A Bad Quaker's Journey** by Ben Stone
17. **Brushfire, A Thriller** by Matthew Wojtecki

Check them out at LibertyUnderAttack.com!

Table of Contents

BONUS: Next Steps (Redux)

More Information

A Note About The Cover Art

The cover is a custom-design by Miriam Zachariah. The idea was to visually represent the merging of the physical and digital Second Realms, the dots on the map being known temporary/permanent autonomous zones (i.e. freedom festivals, van nomad meetups, etc.).

Foreword

A common thread throughout anarchism/libertarianism is the eventual arrival at some utopian, free society. The idea is that if "we" focus "our" efforts on educating individuals on economics, morality, history, etc., "we" can hit critical mass, abolish the State, and live happily ever after. While this "free world" is a pipedream, it doesn't mean that self-liberators can't set up pockets of freedom in the here and now, despite the existence of the State: these respites from First Realm tyranny are called Second Realms.

In *Second Realm: Book on Strategy*, Smuggler and XYZ build upon the framework laid by the likes of Samuel Edward Konkin III, Hakim Bey, and many anonymous cypherpunks: agoras, temporary/permanent autonomous zones, and digital freedom/privacy, respectively. But, the truly unique thing these authors were able to formulate was the merging of the physical and digital realms.

Have you ever been to a freedom festival? Visited a deep web IRC chat? Used I2P (Internet Invisibility Project)? If so, you've seen firsthand the beauty and freedom found within these protected spaces, but you might want to start thinking bigger.

Herein, the authors begin by discussing the underlying philosophy and the motivation for this particular freedom strategy; terms are defined and elaborated upon; they tell you how to practically create Second Realms EVERYWHERE; you'll learn about high and low tech tools that can be used to maintain these realms going into the future; how to facilitate trade between the two realms, and more.

I'd like to provide one disclaimer before turning you over to this book on strategy, though. It's likely that you are already an anarchist looking for solutions. If that's the case, I sincerely believe you will find value in what you are about to read; if not, however, I would highly recommend beginning your anarchist adventure elsewhere – this is not designed to be an introductory book.

In summation, crypto-anarchy has delivered "us" the tools necessary to build Second Realms in cyberspace. While that is a great feat for many reasons, it's important to remember that human beings are social creatures and many individuals long for interaction in physical space and time. Smuggler, XYZ, and their predecessors have given "us" a great starting point.

It's time to start building.

Shane Radliff
December 2018
The Vonu Podcast

Chapter 1: Crypto-Anarchy, Tradecraft, TAZ and Counterculture

This is a booklet for people in search for liberty, and who subscribe to a philosophy of personal, civil, and economic liberty through the absence of government in their lives, along with the presence of strong property rights. Among the varying philosophies that hold this view the most noted is probably that of Anarcho-Capitalism of both the Rothbardian and the Friedmanite flavor. The authors of this booklet subscribe to the former and it is that perspective that should be taken into account to take the most value from this text.

Thanks to Timothy C. May, Hakim Bey, Murray Rothbard, J. Neil Schulman, and Samuel Edward Konkin III for inspiration and ideas to build on.

We also thank "The Free and Unashamed" for asking us to write down our thoughts, and for supporting us in doing so. While you remain a mystery to us, you seem to be a good mystery.

About the authors: This book was written by Smuggler@staff.anarplex.net (smuggler at staff dot anarplex dot net) and "XYZ". We are the sole people responsible. These are our thoughts.

If this booked helped you, gave you pleasure, or just new things to think about, please say "Thank You" by sending us some Bitcoin to:

1DrjUiCT4Wzij8hLYBTYmfPubZMNf2PubU

Chapter 2: Motivation

Anyone subscribing to a radical philosophy of liberty must face the pressing question of how to progress from our current condition of insufficient liberty to a society where individual liberty is respected.

Several strategies for this change have been proposed, ranging from political participation, educating and convincing the masses, civil-disobedience, secession, and counter-economics, to outright revolution.

While these proposals all have some interesting aspects, they are very often naive or poorly informed as to what really shapes society.

The fundamental flaw to most of these strategies, with a slight exception in the theory of counter-economics, is the reliance on mass change of social, cultural, and economic structures and people in general.

It has often been overlooked by voluntaryists that collective thinking dominates many of our personal decision making processes, which is why most of these strategies err by the fallacy of big numbers. By this term, we mean the belief that we must wait for progress until a large number of people rally to the support of our cause.

We disagree, and we think that waiting has been a mistake, and often chosen for the purpose of avoiding risks. We wish to minimize risk, but not to the point of inaction.

Armies of supporters are however not to be expected. The reason for this should be accessible to economists and psychologists alike: Both production and parasitism are natural human strategies to satisfy personal desires.

Both strategies appear naturally and are present within most people (with the exceptions of idealists and moralists on the one hand and outright sociopaths on the other). Both strategies can easily be seen in modern life, with parasitism becoming more profitable with every political intervention.

Our current redistributive society moves property from producers to parasites, as well as shifting decisions from the individual to the ruler. (The ruler, of course, is held above all personal responsibility, recourse, or personal risk.)

A surprisingly large number of people in modern societies are in favor of the redistribution of property, sometimes knowingly and sometimes merely because they regard the rules of the game more than the morals of the game: they see redistribution as the way of the world and work to get "their share."

Parasitism, where enforced by a government, is easier than working. It provides a comparable level of consumption for less effort. In addition, it removes hundreds of daily decisions from an individual, along with the bad feelings of facing mistakes.

It is sadly a truism that most people only want the freedom to be comfortable.

Libertarian class theory describes two classes of people in society: Those that pay more taxes than they consume of public services, and those that consume more public services than they pay taxes. That is: Tax-payers and Tax-feeders.

What is under-appreciated is the size of the second group. In most developing countries, taxfeeders make up far more than a third of the employed, from direct bureaucrats to industries living of public money or regulation. In many developed countries, tax-feeders have approach or passed 50%. (The massive creation of fiat currency has allowed governments to keep this unsustainable game going... so far.) Millions of people profit from this arrangement and will fight to keep it going till the last moment.

If one combines only these two motives for intervening government, redistribution of property, and shifting of decisions, an easy majority of people profit from the existence of such an institution.

There are however additional motives for the existence of the state as a social organization.

One is the identity creating feeling of "belonging" to something - a natural and not always negative motivator of humans. This is regularly exploited by the state to assure support and to limit dissent.

Another motive is the perception of risks and lost opportunities from a change from the current status-quo to a new society solely based on voluntary interaction, contract, and optional law. People feel comfort in the current arrangement and don't want to endure the strain of adapting to a new situation. This is understandable.

The reflexive questions that are instantly asked are ones like these: Who will care for the sick, the old, the children, the environment? Who will build the roads, maintain security, license the doctors, and make sure the trains will be on time?

These questions are often brushed away with a correct, but superficial, reply of "the market." However, this reply is not sufficient. The "market" does not take care of anything - it is merely a system of interaction and exchange. People find solutions to human problems; entrepreneurs spend time and effort to find solutions others will be willing to trade for, and, if they are correct, profit thereby.

Without new supplies of these services (which are generally forbidden by force under the current regimes) the perception of risk cannot be sufficiently countered - certainly not for someone who is agitatedly asking the question so that the frightening possibility of a new human arrangement may be quickly dismissed.

The third motive against change to a voluntary society is the perceived cost of change itself. Aside from adapting to new ways of living, any change will find resistance and risk of failure, ranging from the loss of money or time, to losing life or liberty itself. Very few people are willing to take these risks, and many would be needed to achieve any meaningful change in an entire society.

After all, liberty is costly.

The reasonable conclusion, then, is to cease hoping for large numbers of supporters and instead to focus on strategies that make individual liberty possible in the current situation.

But, while we have ceased hoping for massive events to bring liberty to us, we have not given up hope for liberty - we have merely faced the fact that we'll have to build it brick-by-brick, for ourselves, without waiting for support or permission.

Fortunately, these methods allow us to model a voluntary society for those less willing to take risks, so that a formerly intellectual concept can be shown to them in real life - here and now, to see and feel with no waiting.

This does not require many like-minded people.

The truth is that waiting for consent keeps us from acting. And acting allows us to test and modify our theories in the real world, which is the only way they will ever reach their most useful forms.

Another grave error is often found in the strategic thinking of anarcho-capitalists and voluntaryists.

Since anarcho-capitalism is fundamentally an individual philosophy its adherents are usually staunchly opposed to any notion of collectivism. While in general they are correct, they miss important distinctions in their vehemence.

Collectivism's main tenet is the submission of the individual to the collective - without the individual's express consent.

This includes as much as the individual stepping back, or even being scapegoated, for the "good" of the collective, and the identity of the individual being described chiefly through the terms of the group.

It is critical to emphasize two important aspects of this concept.

First, any membership in a collective does not depend on the express decision of the individual member. He is either forced to be part of it, or at least he is forced to stay part of it after joining.

Second, the identity aspects of a collective are irrelevant in almost all meaningful situations or simply superficial beyond meaning.

We have all seen this in so many forms that it hardly needs a great deal of explanation. What is sometimes under-appreciated, however, is the possibility of collective action by consent.

Voluntaryists and likeminded people have often gone too far in throwing out any kind of social grouping, especially those with the ability to establish identity or culture.

It has often been overlooked that humans often seek out terms and groups that provide them with a means of "belonging to something" as well as "being someone" - not by some magical means of the group itself but because the group is composed of humans that already "belong" or "are."

Group relationships provide a base for forming a culture of common symbols, meanings, ethics and relationships. These are useful, and maybe even necessary, for human social interaction and life.

Furthermore, these groups can form larger societies that provide common institutions, reflect relationships, and simplify interdependencies and allegiances. This leads to increase stability and efficiency of interaction, trade, communication as well as positive identity-establishing functions and more coherent relationships with people outside this society.

It must be emphasized however, that these positive functions of society can only be achieved in groups of voluntary (individually consenting) associations with clear and easy exit-options.

The useful functions of such groups of voluntary associations nourish a culture of liberty and the forming of a "society" of free people increases the attractiveness of anarcho-capitalism by decreasing its image of "coldness", providing a common narrative and establishing a base for voluntary loyalty and allegiance.

These positive aspects open new options to solve some of the problems we face - enforcement of agreements, streamlining of trust-relationships, reputation, mutual aid to name just a few - by learning from methods found in many "primitive" anarchistic societies.

Conclusion

A strategy for the implementation of liberty must be built on three ideas:

1. It is necessary to achieve individual liberty in all aspects - economical, personal, civil - with only a very small subset of the total population. Liberty should be assumed to be a minority position that is actively opposed by some and passively ignored by most. (If ever it becomes more, we'll have no trouble adapting.)

2. All notions of the homogeneity of society, change of mainstream opinion, and universal integrity of a population must be abandoned.

3. We must form a culture and society of liberty, or at least take first steps towards this goal and nourish attempts to accomplish a cultural secession from the mainstream society that allows us to form and protect institutions of social interaction and relationships.

Chapter 3: Introduction

It is rather challenging to write a text about strategy that is both practical and refreshing. Our purpose is to inspire thought, not so much to create a final blueprint. This little book has one purpose: to prepare you for reasonable and effective actions. If you read this but do not act (no matter how much you talk and write,) this book has utterly failed.

Many technologies and methods described in this text already exist and have been tested in real life; others await implementation.

We have been heavily inspired by structures, methods and technologies found with other groups facing the same challenges. This includes organized crime groups like the Triads, Mafia and Yakuza. Our borrowing from them should (obviously) not be understood as an endorsement.

Also, we borrow from various ideas on freedom that came before us, most notably CryptoAnarchy by T. C. May, T.A.Z. by Hakim Bey, as well as Counter-Economics by S.E. Konkin III.

This is a strategy for risk-takers, entrepreneurs and adventurers. Both the risks and the expected rewards are great.

In plain terms: This is not for boys; it is for men. Facing reality is required. Change is created by people with courage, not by the timid who usually follow behind and clamor for credit after all the battles have been fought.

One more thing: The people of courage almost always have the most fun. Enjoy!

Chapter 4: First Steps To Strategy

The first step in formulating a strategy is to achieve clarity about the objectives, means of engagement, obstacles, and resources at our disposal. These four components are interdependent and some of them are subject to constant change (particularly obstacles and resources.)

Objectives are what we hope to accomplish. In this case it is our personal, individual, and exclusive participation in a society where the only legitimate foundation for all interpersonal interaction is that of voluntary agreement.

It is a personal participation because we as physical, mental, and moral beings partake in it with all our aspects, not just in some abstract sense.

It is an individual participation because every member of such a society must decide for himself whether to partake in it or not.

It is exclusive because we prefer to live as part of a voluntary society and not as part of a coercive society.

Means of engagement are the abstract rules that govern our actions in order to achieve our objectives. What actions are permissible and which should be avoided? Since our struggle is an ethical one, our means should be in unison with our objectives, namely to refrain from all nonvoluntary interactions.

This means that the resources we employ must be only be those of our own property, that we abstain from fraud, limit the impact on uninvolved parties, and that we refrain from any violence that is not in self-defense.

Since the claim of self-defense is often abused, another rule should be included as a guideline: To stay away from sources of conflict where we can be falsely accused and to avoid points of conflict where our opponents are likely to attack, requiring violence on our part.

Before we look at the obstacles we face, some notes on our resources will be useful.

From our rules of engagement we are limited to our own bodies, property, and time in achieving our objectives. This puts us into a less fortunate position than our opponents, who can command what they do not own, which is exactly what we are working against. Watering down our rules of engagement in this area would thus result into a weakening of our objectives or even lead to missing them entirely. This has been the case with several historic attempts to create liberty which led to a replacement of the rulers, but not the system of rule, or that used terror to stabilize the new order.

However, using our own resources also allows us to be more flexible in their application since we do not require processes of command and obedience to distribute them. This frees us from complexity and allows for the rapid implementation of tactics.

So, we can expect to be more adaptable than our opponents, so long as we do not introduce new distribution schemes for resources and actions.

We can and should focus on forming an entrepreneurial environment for tactics, and let them refine each other in the marketplace.

But, for a marketplace to work, we must be prepared to reward entrepreneurs for their superior products and services, not just through respect, but also with tangible material considerations (money, etc.).

Contrary to our opponents, our strategy employs the time-tested roles of entrepreneurs, customers, and investors. This is fundamental because it creates a situation in which people who are unable to contribute through the supply of services or products are able to contribute through the investment of time or money in products that will help us all achieve our objectives - and maybe even profit.

What are the obstacles we face? This is an area of much confusion and disagreement. Let us explore this in some depth:

Obstacles

We have already concluded that our objectives are opposed by a majority of the population as well as the ruling class.

It is, however, necessary to analyze the specific methods by which our objectives are opposed and which means are employed to keep us from reaching our goals.

Humans are spatial, social and cooperative beings. We occupy space that no other spatial thing can occupy at the same time. Our bodies need to be somewhere; they need to be sustained.

We are also social because we require interaction with other humans. We want to communicate, we want to learn from each other, we want to procreate. While we are the only thing in the space we occupy, we also need to interact, be viewed, and view other humans around us. We define and achieve social status through interaction and observation and use it to find out how to prevent conflict, to solve conflict when it occurs, to create institutions of interaction and symbols to identify friends and foes, and to optimize our communication.

Since we also live in a scarce world and cannot do every necessary thing alone, we also engage in cooperation, specialization, and trade.

These characteristics of human life constitute the frame for most things we do, but also provide the means for our opponents to keep us in chains.

Throughout history, those that oppose liberty have developed and cultivated a complex and refined "science" on how to keep populations under control. We are not referring to a secretive group of social planners, but a set of techniques that are shared not only by the rulers but by those parts of a society that profit from coercion and the comfort it brings.

To understand this science it is beneficial to look at how our various aspects - spatial, social, and cooperative - are exploited.

It is necessary to understand that the state and the systems of the world are not spatial. Though the state claims geographic control, the state itself cannot occupy any of it, since it is not a physical entity. It is a social concept of control. The only way the state can interact with the spatial is through its agents and proponents, as well as anyone conditioned to represent or call for it.

It is individual humans that must intrude into another individual's space to deliver any kind of force, whether it be direct or indirect.

When not applying force, the only other option for the state to act within space is through its agents, to observe or surveil the space of others.

Cultural norms of the mainstream society and most of its subcultures reward pro-state behavior while they punish non-state behavior. While this is not yet true for all parts of the cultural code, it is increasing, often without us noticing it.

There are numerous examples for this. The method most often suggested for problem-solving is to call the police, to always obey the state authority, to use "convenient" methods of payment (credit cards etc.), to make every payment in official legal tender (national currency), get a "good job", petition your "representatives", "work within the system", pay your "fair share" of taxes, adhere to the current definition of "political correctness", or simply to "not make trouble." All of these codes of conduct focus on a single goal: To integrate into a society that is led, organized, and enabled by the state. Alternative views are quickly labeled "a waste of time", "not practical", "unrealistic", "utopian", "eccentric", or even "treasonous."

Interwoven with these codes are values that most people are accustomed to use when judging their neighbors. While many soldiers today partake in wars that should realistically be called unjust and therefore a crime, they are not met with disgust for choosing this career. Policemen that enforce unethical laws (often with unethical methods) are not excluded from our comradeship, but instead called "our finest." Tax collectors that objectively conduct armed robbery are not called out but identified as "doing their job." In the end, everyone is just following orders.

In addition, a wide variety of symbols are used to identify people as being "respectable." Some of these are: styles of clothing, status symbols, licenses, membership cards, use of language, and laughing at the right time.

Together, these codes, values, and symbols form societal expectations and identities - the function of culture - and any fundamental variation from them is met with rejection or even outright hostility.

It is very important to understand that these codes, values and symbols are highly interconnected and form an integrated body of culture which makes it very hard to successfully break out of this scheme. If we change only parts of it, it is easy to be dragged back into "the old ways" by many parts that are still tied to the larger culture. (Ideally this need not be so, but as a practical matter, it usually is.)

However, breaking away from mainstream culture and its various subcultures leaves the dissenter as a tolerated eccentric at best, or an unwanted troublemaker at worst. But it also puts the individual in the position of having no social integration... which is required by most of us simply for mental survival.

But worse than this, is being removed from cooperative functions of society. Many institutions of our society were originally created to streamline cooperation between individuals. Since then, however, they have been taken-over and remodeled to support state dominion.

These institutions are numerous and we will only list the most important ones here:

- Money and banking systems

- Property titles
- Identity (papers, passports, etc.)
- Licenses, regulations and insurance
- Law enforcement and security
- Legal system, courts, correction and punishment
- Education and media
- Communication, Energy and transportation networks
- Charity (now welfare)

Each of these institutions and services are tightly controlled by the state. Access and provision are limited to those that are not perceived as enemies of the system and those that follow cultural norms.

These systems are necessary for successful cooperation between individuals; to satisfy the needs they cannot satisfy alone.

It is by regulation, licensing, and cultural dominance that access to, and the provision of, these institutions and services is regulated, always with a tight integration of surveillance and punishment. Though there are always cracks in this control that allow people to slip through, the main occupation for legislators and bureaucrats appears to search for and close those cracks - to create a system in which these institutions, combined with a matching culture, provide a totalitarian toolset and mold each individual under the dominance of the state system.

Cultural codes, values, symbols, and systems and institutions of cooperation enable the state to become a spatial entity, through its agents, proponents and dependents. Culture forms the base for active consent while access control of institutions creates a soft force to keep the subjects in line. (The benefits of compliance outweigh the risks of dissent.)

This supplies the state with the individual people that project its force into the spatial realm through their actions. This starts with simple social exclusion of dissenters, continues with snitching and inviting the state agents into situations where they are unwanted, and ends by using force against dissenters.

The interwoven aspects of culture, institutions, profits from redistribution and the longing for stability form the foundation of the power of states and assure lasting consent (both passive and active) for this system of domination.

We call the totality of this system: The First Realm.

Please keep in mind that we are here talking about the system of domination, not the specific implementation or parties running it.

Thus far, attempts to change this system have (at most) changed the faces running the show, but have never fundamentally changed the game.

Although we may call the population's support for this system unethical, misguided, stupid, or even evil, it is nevertheless a reality that must be faced clearly.

Our challenge is of an enormous magnitude. This is why previous strategies have failed to achieve much lasting change.

Conclusions

We can thus draw the following conclusions:

1. Spatial: We have to find or create territory (space) in which no agent, proponent, or dependent of the state is present or can deliver force in any direct manner. With the exception of outer space (and maybe the high seas), it is unlikely that any territory that is not preoccupied by agents of the state can currently be found. There is no point in trying to create such a territory.

2. Spatial: We have to protect and defend the territory of liberty against state surveillance. Surveillance is the precursor to force, whether direct or indirect. (Otherwise, what purpose does it have?)

3. Spatial: We must minimize the need of free men to enter territory that is occupied by agents of the state or surveilled by them.

4. Institutional: It is required to form independent systems of cooperation that are formed on the ethics of liberty and that are not dependent upon or connected to institutions of control (masquerading as institutions of cooperation).

5. Institutional: We cannot rely on any state dominated institution to form the basis of our interactions or our own systems.

6. Institutional: Any interaction with state controlled institutions must happen by proxy and with the uttermost separation, to limit any damage that can (and will) occur.

7. Cultural: We need to create and nurture our own culture based on the values defined by the ethics of liberty.

8. Cultural: Our culture cannot be a simple sub- or counter-culture to the state dominated mainstream culture. It must be an independent counter-culture.
9. Cultural: We require our own cultural symbols for mutual recognition to optimize communication and social ordering, as well as to support separation from the culture of our opponents.
10. Cultural: The cultural codes and norms of liberty must support both the integration and nurturing of free men and the exclusion of state agents.

Our strategy for liberty is the creation of a culture of liberty, a society that occupies its own protected space and implements independent systems of cooperation. We need to create a Second Realm.

This task may justly be seen as monumental and the stakes are high. However, it is most definitely attainable. Several groups have achieved these precise objectives in the past and were often able to sustain their systems for centuries. The only major difference between those successful cultural entrepreneurs and free men is that we are more restrained in our rules of engagement. Nonetheless, even this can be used as a lasting advantage.

Anarchy is the free grouping of men into societies of their preference.

Chapter 5: The Second Realm

After having defined the boundaries and the objectives of a necessary strategy - the creation of a Second Realm - it is time to look into the implementation.

Several past and existing groups serve as inspiration to us in imagining of a future for free men. However, they should not serve as blueprints; only as examples to learn from. We will have to do things no one has done before.

As an inspirational excursion, let us look at several of these examples:

Organized crime groups: Everyone knows the Italian mafia, the Yakuza, Triads, and outlaw motorcycle gangs from news coverage. What is often overlooked is that these organizations are not simple chaotic gangs, but often exhibit a long history and their own kind of society.

The mafia, as an example, is primarily a loose knit network of independent gangs that pay tribute to their dons and receive protection and their own conflict-resolution system in return. Their aim is to limit conflict within groups and not resort to violence when other means of conflict resolution are available. They operate their own title system of territories and markets, they provide services for communication and reputation, and they foster the division of labor through specialization. One could define the mafia as an organized crime business association based on a shared ethical background.

Similarly the Triads are built on ethnicity (Han Chinese) and sharing a cultural narrative (resistance to the Manchu rule). They have been around for centuries, mostly by establishing an integrated society and trying to limit their activities to inter-triad conflict, exploiting street criminals, and focusing on less-public crime.

A similar pattern of social narrative, ethnic focus, and well controlled intervention into the public realm shows itself with the Yakuza. They even put a strong focus on being recognizable by the public.

While the previous three examples cover older organizations, outlaw motorcycle gangs are a more recent phenomenon. They openly display their outlaw image as part of their culture, create their own social norms, and use their own form of justice.

All of the previous examples share some characteristics in operation and organization that can serve as hints to what successful parallel structures need.

First, they are all based on their own independent culture and values. They are not chaotic and "lawless", but have their own laws that are often stricter and more conservative than mainstream culture. For example, the Yakuza forbid their members to partake in theft, the Mafia punishes members for adultery, and all of them take oaths and vocal contracts very seriously.

Another common characteristic is that these groups usually try to limit violence to their own community instead of spreading chaos. This has two reasons: Obviously this limits the attention of law enforcement and public opinion that could make their business harder, but these people also understand themselves as being part of their local community, which they often take effort to protect and help. This has the positive side-effect of gaining public support within their territorial presence.

Contrary to popular opinion, these groups are not hierarchical command-and-control structures. Sub-groups are often autonomous and do not follow top-down planning. Instead, they share part of their profit with the upper hierarchy in return for specialized services, investment, and justice provision. Often these groups have to answer to their leaders primarily for causing too much trouble, being too violent, or interfering with other sub-group's business. Apart from that, they are highly independent.

The last commonality to point out is that these groups control locations like club-houses, offices, restaurants, or similar places where they can meet and conduct their business outside of public view and which they protect against surprise raids or infiltration by round-the-clock staffing, alarms, posts, guards, and security technology.

Surely these groups conduct business that is highly unethical and employ methods that conflict with the rules of engagement we are limited to, nevertheless they also provide some hints for long term stability of outlaw organizations. These are:

1. They define and nurture their own parallel culture and society.
2. They follow a least-intervention policy concerning outsiders, especially in the realms of violence.

3. Local autonomy for sub-groups protects them against decapitation and maximizes their flexibility.
4. They create a positive image in their local community through acts of aid and relief.
5. Temporary autonomous locations provide them with protected spaces to conduct their business. These locations often exist long enough to justify them as semi-permanent.
6. Using specialization and division of labor, they create an internal market for the provision of common services required throughout their sub-groups.
7. They all have a high focus on operating their own independent internal justice systems and legal code.
8. Because of their outlaw nature they have to maintain their own security and defense operations against other outlaw organizations that intrude on their turf or prove hostile.

We can see that these groups are faced with similar problems to those we face - spatial, cultural and institutional - and they have developed ways of meeting these challenges.

Below, some of these solutions are explored in detail and adapted to our specific obstacles, resources, and rules of engagement. Furthermore, some additional and necessary components for the Second Realm are presented. Together, these form the foundation of a workable model for the parallel society we require.

Chapter 6: Temporary Autonomous Zones Revised

Though this is doing some violence to Hakim Bey's original definition, a Temporary Autonomous Zone is a space or territory that temporarily eludes the control of a generally recognized government.

There are several examples of this which differ in their autonomy or duration, from wholly independent permanent zones to only short lived simulated autonomy.

The oldest of these examples can be found in middle-ages Europe in the form of Ghettos which not only served as a place to concentrate "unwanted" social groups, but gave those groups internal autonomy in form of their own tax and justice systems. Most important in this respect are the ghettos of the Jewish diaspora.

Another example can be found today in Latin America where favelas not only are excluded from receiving official government services but also constitute permanent autonomous zones in which government force plays a rule only during high-level raids, but not on a daily basis. In the same category we find squatted skyscrapers in several Latin American cities that have not been entered by any state agent for official functions for years.

Kowloon Walled City was another example of such a semi-permanent autonomous zone until its demolition in 1993. Located in unclaimed territory at the border of British Hong Kong, with a footprint of roughly a third of a square kilometer, it had been a largely ungoverned place since about 1950 and was home to over 33,000 people.

This concept and the various examples of its real-life implementation are of enormous importance to our strategy, being one of the primary solutions for the spatial problem.

Temporary Autonomous Zones give us the opportunity for our culture in exist physical space, allowing us to conduct our business, organize our social relationships, and to handle conflicts in the way we think to be right.

However, our autonomous zones are sometimes too limited in time. We need to follow a "foreign policy" that increases their duration and makes them safe places for social and business activities.

For this there exist two general methods. The first involves a Temporary Autonomous Zone being set up in secret, hidden from the attention of the surrounding state. While this can work for a while, it is very limited, since eventually the place will become known and additional means of stability required. The second method focuses on reaching an "informal toleration" by state authorities. For this such a zone must meet three criteria:

First, the zone may not become a nuisance for neighbors nor be known as the source for trouble for people and property outside the zone. This specifically includes that the property rights of the territory must be respected and an agreement reached with the owners before conducting any autonomous activities there. Any justification for third-party influence must be prevented.

Second, the zone and its inhabitants must strictly adhere to the principle "what happens in the zone stays in the zone," meaning that all conflict must be solved without the intervention of outside law enforcement. This implies that internal trouble-makers have to be dealt with immediately before conflicts can escalate. In addition, state agents and proponents must be discouraged from visiting the place. Usually this happens by not inviting persons of questionable reputation or known friends of the state.

Third, the cost of intervention by any outside party must be increased so much that it becomes unjustified, and that it is more profitable for the attacker to look the other way. While bribes are a common method to reach this goal, a further tactic promises success:

Conceal, Know, Delay, Defend, Destroy, Recover.[1]

First, conceal any information about what happens within the zone from outside surveillance. This requires the employment of access control to keep potential threats from entering the area as well as countermeasures against signals surveillance from within and especially from the outside. For example, such a place should not have attributable communication lines connecting it to the world but instead use anonymization technology to conceal the content and source of its communication. Furthermore, the area should not be observable from the outside and special attention should be given to watch for surveillance attacks.

Second, one needs to know when a physical attack - a raid - against the place is in preparation or ongoing. This requires ways to keep an eye on the surroundings and to have an alarm system that can warn everyone within the area that an attack is imminent.

Third, delaying the attacker with passive means to prevent him from successfully executing a surprise attack. This usually involves multiple barriers, such as several reinforced doors that need to be broken through before the main area of interest can be reached. This is necessary to enable the current occupants of the temporary autonomous zone to:

Fourth, defend the place. While this is optional against a state attacker it will become a necessity against raids by non-state actors like gangs and other kinds of violent organized crime that hope to find valuables or claim territory. In case of non-state actors, defense by deterrence can prove profitable. This can be done by displaying that both alarm-systems and ways of delaying are present, for example CCTV systems and barbed wire barriers.

Next, any attacker must always be unsuccessful in reaching the objective of his attack. This usually means that anything that could be of interest to the attacker must be destroyed or removed. This serves a double purpose. On the one hand it discourages the attacker and others after him from attacking such an area again because the cost of attack surpasses any profit gained from it. On the other hand, it serves to keep any valuable information from the attackers. It keeps them away from anything that could be used to either plan future attacks or serve as evidence in trials against zone occupants. In the case of black market activities the product must be separated from the merchant so that ownership cannot be proven and the merchant prosecuted. For this to be successful, anti-surveillance measures must be taken seriously.

Last, it is necessary to not give up the strategy after the first successful attack. Any operation must be committed to recover to be stable in the long term. While "scare-off" attacks can be profitable for the attacker if the strategy is dropped afterwards, repeated attacks quickly become problematic in regards to both cost and public opinion.

It is very important to emphasize that we are not talking about a "military compound" that has been created to fend off an attack. Instead the goal of our proposal is to create areas that make successful repeat attacks for profit or evidence very costly and less attractive. Any kind of direct, open battle with state actors will lead to defeat and loss of life and freedom. Instead, our goal is to keep evidence out of the hands of the attackers. The only situation in which a stand-off can be profitable is against non-state violent criminals.

For our purposes, such a temporary autonomous zone can range from business clubs of a semi-permanent nature to street markets that only last a few hours. The security requirements for different kinds of zones may differ significantly according to the risks they face. For most operations a well run restaurant with a back room and 24/7 staff can be sufficient. In any case the tactical principles mentioned above should be kept in mind.

The primary purpose of a temporary autonomous zone in our strategy remains to **"keep evidence out of the hands of attackers, and to have a secure place for our culture and business."**

As further inspiration, these zones can serve as not just as a place of social activity, but also for protection of goods and places of business. Another example for its use are trading-posts where one-to-one business that has to be conducted in person takes place, or temporary autonomous markets that open merchant activity to our sub-society. Furthermore, these places can be used as Agadir - traditional installations to store valuables securely.

Additional methods for operating those places can be explored, but they are purely tactical and specific to the use in question. Thus we leave them as an exercise to the reader and to other publications.

Chapter 7: Beyond Physicality – Towards Information

One of the greatest advantages of Temporary Autonomous Zones is the ability to live as if you are free - because you are, at least at that place and time.

This advantage is not only true for physical places, but also for digital places. While the term "digital place" is misleading because the physicality of the digital realm is negligible, it can nevertheless serve some of the same purposes that a physical TAZ can fulfill.

Creating a digital autonomous zone, a permanent digital autonomous zone, allows us to socialize, communicate and trade within an environment that can be highly protected against third party involvement and coercion through the use of technology and cryptography.

Here people can talk to each other as if the state did not exist, they can prepare or even conduct trades without having to spend a single thought on the legal realm their physical body resides in. A large portion of our life that is not tolerated by the surrounding society can be conducted in the safety of cypherspace.[2]

Since anonymizing technology and cryptography can separate our coercible body from our acting mind and identity, we have the ability to experiment with new cultural, social, and legal forms here - without the risk of being locked up in jail or being scoffed at.

That said, digital autonomous zones cannot replace the spatial aspects of our humanity. It is hard to have a drink in cyberspace, you cannot look into each others' faces during a negotiation, and only digital goods can be transacted directly. When we combine digital and physical autonomous zones, the best of the two worlds can be combined: using digital technology for negotiations and ad-hoc meetings while using physical autonomous zones to hand over the goods or to have the drink together. This is crucial for social binding. Often, the riskiest parts of a transaction - handing over the money and enforcing contracts - can be transferred to cypherspace where protection is assured through the use of very strong mathematics. We will go into some of the necessary technologies below.

Combining physical and digital autonomous zones thus provides us with a wide array of protection methods that allow us to act freely, because we are free.

The Future

The full impact of autonomous zones will show itself in the near future. Technologies are changing optimal business sizes and the number and diversity of products and actors required for a functioning market. At this time it is difficult for us to be self-sufficient in our free zones. In the future we will not only have the ability to be self-sufficient if we want to, but we may be forced to rely much more on ourselves due to social collapse in the First Realm.

There are several technologies and economic trends that should be kept on the radar of any anarcho-capitalist.

Two of these technologies are the advent of various kinds of urban farming, especially industrial vertical urban farming (which promises to make food-production for many thousand consumers possible and economical - in a single skyscraper) and micro-fabbing. Micro-fabbing is the automated production of parts through means of 3D-printing without the need of special tool development. This will allow the download of construction plans from the internet and subsequent printout of complex geometries with 3D-printers that do not require any attention during production. The number of base materials available for this method is increasing rapidly and will soon permit anyone with the right skills to compete with specialized, high-capital production facilities, with a fraction of both risk and investment.

These and other technologies reinforce a trend that can be seen in growing parts of the western economies, and that is the move from a mass-consumer culture to a pro-sumer culture in which many more people are self-employed, artisans' shops return to the urban environment and mass products lose their charm.

When we combine autonomous zones with changes in economic and technological fields, as well as changes in social composition, it is easy to envision micro-territories becoming attractive again. This will be the great opportunity for us to sow the seeds of liberty into growing parts of the population without falling for the fallacy of masses. But, for this to be successful, our activities have to begin far in advance. We must show models that can be built upon and structures that have already weathered a few storms. Our model should be seen as proven, workable, or even attractive.

Chapter 8: A Few Thoughts on Securing Trade – Tradecraft Basics

There is little question that trade - and any other social interaction - must be protected against third party intrusion by coercion, theft, or similar violation. We are faced with an additional threat simply because we exist and interact outside the system that the host-state permits us.

This threat is rooted in our opposition to the justice provision mandated by the state.

On the one hand we are unable to use the state's justice system as a remedy against violations we experience from outsiders, which requires us to have our own means of defending against third party aggression and achieve justice if that defense fails. We need our own justice system and enforcement mechanisms.

On the other hand, the state's justice system and law enforcement branches are opposed to the existence of our systems and the actions we partake in outside their claimed realm. We thus face the state trying to intrude into our affairs and to punish us for not obeying him or hiding from his agents.

The latter problem - persecution by the state - deserves some extra thought. How do we protect ourselves against an opponent that powerful?

Let us introduce a few concepts here that can help us design methods to counter this threat.

Pseudonymity. One of the methods of control that are used by our opponents that permeate the mainstream culture and is tight into most institutions of cooperation is the use of "True Names" - our official, state sanctioned, widely known identity of which each of us shall only have one, and which ties all of our actions together. Surely having and using names is a requirement in many social and commercial interactions. Without it we cannot easily find each other again, address each other, or have a history that enables others to assess us.

However, there is no inherent necessity for these names to be the ones our parents gave us at birth, or to be underwritten by the state, or even that each one of us carries only one name at one time and forever.

Pseudonymity is the concept of having alternative names and identities that we reveal as they are needed, that are attached to their own histories and reputations. Breaking the spell of our "True Name" and using self-chosen, task specific identities enables us to limit the ability of our opponents to attach all our actions to the leash that binds us to them and at the same time utilize the functions that names and identities provide. These pseudonyms do not need to be registered by the state nor do they need to be tied to our true identity as long as specific methods of assurance and enforcement are available.

Anonymity. Contrary to modern propaganda, there is nothing wrong with anonymity per se. Many of our actions and trades do not need to be revocable nor do they have the ability to cause any significant harm to others. In these cases it is perfectly fine to not have any name or identity at all. Given the right structure of interaction, there is no need for attribution at all.

The most prominent example for an area where anonymity is practical and useful is in digital communication. While we might chose to be pseudonymous for the parties we want to be known by, all other parties should not know who is acting. For those latter parties we stay anonymous.

Opaqueness. Most of us have been trained to view any secret and non-transparency as a dire threat. Thinking about this should quickly reveal that such a broad opposition to secrets is an idiocy, lacking any justification. Due to the totalitarian tendencies of mainstream culture and political organization - the desire to control others - secrets have become a thing to abhor.

Secrets themselves are never a problem, it is the fraud and coercion they could hide that are the source of danger. When we design our systems in such a way that the parties directly and voluntarily involved are the only ones that can be affected in any relevant way, it becomes clear that those parties can keep a secret for themselves against all other parties that are not directly involved.

Thus opaqueness of action in relation to non-affected parties can protect us from third-party intervention and punishment without inviting additional dangers. There is no justification for anyone but buyer and seller to know who is selling what to whom. No one needs to know what person A tells person B if no other person's justified interest is at peril.

Since we have used the word "justified" or "justification" repeatedly above, let us be clear what it means: Our knowledge of actions - or our involvement in them - is only justified if they involve our property or conflicting agreements we have with any of the acting parties. **Anything that does not involve either of these - property or contract - is simply none of our business.**

Hiding actions and information from the view of third parties prevents them from gaining an information advantage that can be used against us - either by collecting evidence or by discovering leads that enable them to intervene in later situations.

Untraceability. While this is a special case of opaqueness and thus already covered before it deserves some specific mention. Untraceability refers to the function that the movement of an object from one owner or possessor to another, from one location to another or from one condition to another remains hidden from any party not justly required to have this information.

This keeps attackers from discovering information by linking various trades or pieces of information together and thus again serves to minimize evidence that can be collected by them or leads to be followed.

Compartmentalization. Again, it is the all too present totalitarian and collectivist attitude that lurks within our subconscious that brought us busybodies, command-and-control hierarchies and a quirky feeling when we are neither asked for our permission nor involved in everything - even if we have no justified need to be included.

Instead, we should begin to appreciate individual initiative and the competition of ideas and solutions without everything being centrally or collectively planned, widely reported and neatly synchronized. While our human curiosity longs for input, it is often more profitable to separate our actions from those of others in such a way that an outside third party is kept from seeing the whole picture or piecing enough together to act against us.

Deniability. If all previous efforts to keep our opponents from getting a clear picture of what we do fail, it is necessary to at least keep them from using this information against us as individuals. This is where deniability comes in and also puts all other methods into context. Being able to plausibly deny our involvement in a specific action hinders a third party from confidently pointing the finger at us so we can escape damage when everything else has failed.

The concepts introduced above - Deniability, Opaqueness, Untraceability, Compartmentalization, Anonymity and Pseudonymity[3] - applied in that order, are the antidote to the imaginary omniscience of our opponents. Instead of dispersing information far and wide and leaving behind traces with any move, the foundation is **Need to Know**.

It is necessary to limit information to the bare minimum required for the invited and affected parties. The information justly required can of course differ from case to case, but uninvited and unaffected parties should always be prevented from acquiring any meaningful information or deducing potentially harmful conclusions. The art of implementing the objectives of "Need to Know" is commonly known as **tradecraft**.

Using the strategy of minimized information comes with some risks of its own.

First, it can be counterproductive for social cohesion within our subculture and social groups. This requires us to not have paranoia rule us and security to become a religion. One countermeasure against this risk is specialization described in the next section.

The second risk is that we overlook that sometimes evidence is required for the feasibility of our internal justice system. There are two remedies against this. One is that we must design methods of interaction that drastically limit the potential for criminal or otherwise harmful behavior. Some of these methods are mentioned further below.

Another way is to recall that evidence does not have to be publicly available without a party announcing that wrongdoing took place. We can design our systems in such a way that only affected parties can make recourse to evidence revealed on demand so that it can be presented in mediation or arbitration proceedings.

It is up to us to redesign ways of interaction based not on collectivist thought but on individual responsibility. While this may sound impossible, it is not. Many of these methods and processes were been in use before strong states and collectivist culture took over - we just have to rediscover them.

Specialization

Successfully applying tradecraft presents us with two challenges that need to be satisfied. On the one hand, as mentioned above, too much tradecraft can be counterproductive to social cohesion and organization. On the other hand, successful tradecraft is an art that is not easy to master for everyone in every situation.

The solution for these challenges is specialization. Entrepreneurs can excel in providing tradecraft services to other actors in the marketplace by providing means of covert communication, opaque trading-rooms, un-traceable transportation or insured pseudonyms.

This frees other actors from having to unduly invest into these abilities and keeps a culture of paranoia from seeping into everything we do. However, specialization cannot serve as excuse for anyone to ignore this subject or drop the awareness for its necessity.

Another area unique to our situation is the integration into the larger economy. Since a sufficient market-size and diversity can only be hoped for on the long run, we are required to interact and integrate with other markets unless we want to find ourselves in a subsistence economy. However, this integration comes with great risk.

These facts call for a special career that is especially interesting to people that have not yet found their vocation (or who have left their previous vocation) and are looking for low capital opportunities: The Proxy-Merchant.

A proxy-merchant is a bridge connecting the Second Realm to the First Realm while keeping risks at bay. Many ways of bridge-building are conceivable, from people who handle exchanges between Second Realm money and official currencies to shopping and trading agents. We leave it to the reader to invent his own niche.

Chapter 9: Security and Defense

Let's face it: Both the First and the Second Realm are not flower meadows where nothing can go wrong and only peaceful and well-meaning people roam.

While most people most of the time are not violent and do not personally partake in robbery (most simply outsource it to the tax-man), there are some that resort to force to achieve their goals.

In the eyes of the First Realm the Second Realm is outlaw territory inhabited by outlaws - and that is exactly the view other outlaws will have as well. We cannot and should not resort to First Realm protection and security "services" lest we give up our independence. Therefore it is necessary that we provide these services ourselves and develop a mindset to counter this challenge. Since this subject cannot be covered completely within this book we will only give it some thought and invite entrepreneurs in this area to follow up.

Security starts with keeping the peace. While this might sound obvious it is nevertheless often forgotten. Keeping the peace means that one is active in not starting trouble and to stay out of harm's way before a conflict can start or escalate. We must refrain from provoking others to attack us by the behavior we display. It starts with not employing violence ourselves unless it happens in self-defense, not defrauding others, not breaking agreements, not bragging and challenging. Quietness, integrity, and honesty combined with confidence reduces the risk of conflict greatly.

To be only passive, however, does not help. Successful defense starts with preparedness and preemptive action. This not only includes the setup of defensive installations, but also the choice of location and especially the active limitation of hostile intelligence gathering by potential adversaries.

Furthermore, it is profitable to employ low-profile counter-intelligence activities to develop an overview of potential threats and the ability to detect actions against us before they strike.

Choice of location for our temporary autonomous zones is a crucial task. Three factors shall be emphasized here.

First, our installations and property can be inviting for aggressors or uninteresting to them. A big sign saying "outlaw territory for rich capitalists" is a bad idea, but more subtle attributes can also lead to trouble.

Second, the first line of defense is access control. Every club-owner knows that good bouncers keep nuisances away. Being careful about who enters our places drastically reduces the risk of bad surprises.

Third, paths of approach to a protected place need to be known, observed, and controlled. Knowing that an attack is imminent and being able to both delay the attacker as well as the number of directions he can attack from puts one in a vastly better position than presenting oneself on a silver tray. To give an almost perfect example for such a place, let us describe a private club that is located in a major city in Europe.[4]

The club rooms are on the top floor of a 20-something story skyscraper in the commercial district. There are three ways to get to the place - an elevator, two emergency staircases, and the helipad on the roof.

The elevator and the staircases are guarded by security personal during the club's business hours and equipped with a CCTV system controlled from within the club's perimeter. The only way to enter the rooms for a regular visitor is to call the club while waiting at the elevator on ground floor, and if access is granted, the elevator is sent down with a lift-boy that has to unlock the top-floor with a key.

The floor below is an office with different business hours that is integrated into the club's alarm system.

In case of a raid, the attackers can be delayed for several minutes while everyone within the club is notified immediately. Potential troublemakers can be repelled far away from the protected zone. This keeps the place peaceful while allowing anyone to take necessary steps before the attackers enter the place. Ideally, some evacuation procedures involving the helipad could be implemented. Any surprise attack short of total annihilation is close to impossible.

This is of course a very elaborate and expensive operation, but it can serve as inspiration for our own.

For more information, please go back to the section about Temporary Autonomous Zones.

What if an attack really takes place? As already mentioned above, the defense against a state actor can only consist of slowing him down, or temporarily fending him off. One cannot win against a huge state - only die trying. All one can do is to limit the impact of a raid by separating evidence from the persons at risk (Deniability) and by escaping and later recovering.

In case of another outlaw attacking, a serious cost-benefit analysis has to take place and lead to an active, victory-oriented defense. Before anyone's thoughts run amok here, let us be clear that we are not talking about waging war including counter-attacking the adversary on its own territory. It is about limiting harm, not big victories and history book coverage.

Without going too deep into the subject, it is worth noticing that the question of coordinated defense is harder for an individualistic society than for a collectivist.

The reason for this is that defense is a numbers-game. The number, strength, and preparation of the forces involved as well as the ability to quickly coordinate decide about the success of any kind of standoff. This does require individuals to delegate leadership of the forces one joins - something few of us are prepared or willing to do. However, thinking deeply about the issue at hand can serve as preparation for this. Effective defense is based on mobility and flexibility, the dynamic grouping, regrouping, dispersing of actors as well as the on-demand centralization and decentralization of command at the required level of hierarchy.

It is necessary to develop strategies in this area that are known to those that commit to partake in these actions - should they be required - so that the individual consent to supporting and partaking can be assured and a realistic estimate of available resources is possible.

From the above it should be obvious that this is an area of specialization where entrepreneurs can make their living, as it is already done today. It should also be obvious that these services need to be actually bought by us and not ignored.

To inspire potential entrepreneurs in this industry who want to be active in the Second Realm, two technologies shall be presented that promise to be useful in our specific situation:

Anonymized Remote Controlled Access Control

One day there will be a banging on the door leading to one of our protected places: "Police, we have a search warrant." Now is the time for the ice-cold Second Realm security provider to prove what he is worth. Sheepishly pressing the button to immediately open the door and putting everyone inside into peril, or doing nothing except sending out a warning to everyone and letting the attackers work their way through the concrete reinforced gate. The combination of remote CCTV perimeter control and communication anonymity greatly reduces the potential consequences for the remote bouncer and gives him the freedom to act in the interest of his customers. To further add security, multiple anonymous operators located at different unknown locations could be required to agree on an action so that neither infiltration, bribery, blackmail, nor pure fear can undermine the security of the temporary autonomous zone.

Anonymized Remote Controlled Defense Systems

In a future further away, the previous access control systems can be extended to incorporate active less-lethal defense systems. The currently available robotic weapons platforms similar to those that are used at the intra-Korean border could in the future be integrated into the arsenal of specialized TAZ-defense contractors. Again, anonymous communication and remote sensors are the foundation but this time extended by random task assignment to anonymous off-location operators so that it becomes impossible for any third party to find proof of who pulled the trigger to fend off the attacking street gang.

Contrary to what most people are used to, security is nothing that can only be left to the experts and professionals, even though the security and defense industry provides specialized services. To preserve long-term autonomy it is necessary to counter-balance the power any security and defense provider can accumulate. While one should be prepared to procure security services on the market, and thus pay for them, it is also necessary to have a counter-weight for worst case scenarios in which a security provider attempts to monopolize his position.

The time-tested method is to not give up one's own preparedness and abilities of defense. Everyone should be prepared to resist a security provider, willing to do so as soon as it is necessary, and to be eternally vigilant to not let such a potential threat slip our attention. This does of course require coordinated action by many since a single person will not be able to contain such a danger alone. Therefore it must be part of our culture to keep a watchful eye on those we pay to defend us. Remember: It is crucial for the lasting liberty and stability of the Second Realm that everyone is willing, watchful, and able to withstand attempts by security providers to monopolize their industry.

Do not let yourself be scared off by the previous section. Active defense measures are commonplace and often go unnoticed to most people. Be it the club-scene, red-light industry, or bouncers - most of the time nothing happens, and most of the remaining times only minor quarrels take place. Life is different from what is shown on TV. In most less-developed countries the provision of personal and group defense is commonplace since the state does not bother protecting one outlaw against the other, or the public against the outlaws.

Being prepared, and attackers knowing that you are, takes most of the risk out of the game. This is true for any potential aggressor - state or not. Let us hope that preparation is enough.

Chapter 10: The Blessings of Technology

Many of the tasks we are confronted with seem to be impossible to solve at first glance. And just a few decades ago that would have been a correct assessment. Luckily for us, technological advantages of the last thirty years open new opportunities.

Two areas in which technology can help us shall be explored in the following.

The oppression by the First Realm forces us to employ methods to conceal our actions and to leave no evidence behind.

- **Anonymous communication technologies** - many of which are available right now - allow us to send and receive messages, surf the web, and offer digital services in a way that neither sender nor recipient can be identified by third parties.

- **Dark-net systems** give us the leverage we need to operate our own access controlled and anonymous communication networks as an inconspicuous overlay of the Internet.

- **Encryption** allows us to send messages only intended recipients can read.

- **Digital signatures** enable us to digitally sign contracts in unforgeable ways so that remote and pseudonymous trading can be implemented.

- **Anonymous untraceable digital cash** makes our transactions invisible to outsiders and breaks any attempt to freeze all of our assets or identify the volume or parties of our trades.

- **Mobility and remoteness** empowers us to act without being physically present, thus removing operators from environments of high threat and making things like secure counter-surveillance, blackmail resistant physical access control, and physical trading machines possible.

- **Secret sharing and secret splitting** give us opportunities to distribute decisions and secrets over many parties that can only act when a predefined threshold of agreement is reached. This can be used to both create secure escrow systems and strong pseudonyms that are able to bear long-term reputation.

- **Distributed consent**, the ability to trigger an action only if remote, often anonymous, predefined parties agree on the action. This makes coercion, blackmail, and sting operations against us much harder, while giving the involved parties plausible deniability.

- **Geo-caching** offers some solutions for physical trades in which the selling party is at risk. Placing the goods at a hidden location and communicating the coordinates to the buyer afterwards allows goods to travel without both parties having to meet.

However, these technologies come with a downside when we have to enforce contracts and detect fraud in our groups. Our mindset on creating evidence for mediation and arbitration cases as well as the enforceability of contracts has to change.

Bonded escrows are schemes where the maximum penalty that could occur in a fraudulent trade needs to be insured with a party of high reputation or reachability. This allows us to enforce contracts even if one or more parties involved disappear in the fog of anonymity after committing their crimes, making fraud uneconomical.

Unique tamperproof security seals that are hard to forge and are destroyed on tampering combined with timestamped video recording and various challenge-and-response schemes enable us to create very secure evidence in case we have to prove that a good meets the agreed on quality and quantity. Combined with bonded escrow and geo-cached delivery it is one of many schemes to anonymously trade goods without putting the seller at risk of capture nor the buyer at risk to be defrauded.

As a general rule we need to find methods to create evidence necessary for potential conflict resolution processes without giving away identity to uninvited third parties. Several of these methods have already been found, but it is not the purpose of this book to get into too much detail but to demonstrate the feasibility of this strategy and inspire people to find their own solutions in the tactical arena.

Chapter 11: Shared Services

In the First Realm the following is called "institutional services" and only provided "officially" and with licenses to legitimize the control exercised. Institutions become social organisms on their own, insulating themselves against competition and abolishment.

In the Second Realm, competition, diversity, and choice are the norm, which is why we call these "Shared Services."

Life itself and especially a strategy of active opposition comes with a variety of risks. While many of these risks can be limited or mitigated, living and acting completely without taking risk is impossible. Only people of independent wealth are able to face these risks on their own - or at least believe that they can.

It is crucial that we create solutions for this problem by establishing **networks of mutual aid**. There are two reasons for this:

First, we have to enable people to not fall back into state controlled welfare systems in case of disaster. Liberty requires separation from the state in these areas as well: "To be free, the slave must first refuse the master's gruel."

Contrary to the offers of the state, this area needs to be covered by entrepreneurs and mutual aid agreements on a social level. Helping out our friends in need while at the same time encouraging and helping them to help themselves again should be the goal. If this is reached best by commercial operations or on a social level remains to be discovered - by the marketplace. However, nothing on the market happens without for-profit or social entrepreneurs acting and implementing solutions.

Since we are confronted by oppression by the state, a unique set of risks asks to be faced and handled. Some of the things we do might lead to individuals facing the wrath of the First Realm, be it imprisonment or asset forfeiture. To enable people to take the required steps, risk sharing in form of insurances for our businesses is required. This can happen on a low level of "emotional support" by **visiting prisoners**, or better even to help out with lawyer's fees and economic support for the families at home. Apart from the increased ability of individuals to take more risks it also helps by providing additional social cohesion. However, care should be taken to not encourage people to take risks indiscriminately or to become solely dependent on the support provided to them by the Second Realm society.

Internal justice systems are another example of shared services. We are not going to progress into a utopian future where fraud, theft, and aggression disappear. Instead we have to find ways to provide conflict resolution, enforcement, and restitution systems.

This requires ways to securely register contracts and retain evidence in case of future disagreements without risking that uninvited third parties gain any information.

Using these **contract-registries** and **evidence-retention systems**, affected parties can call on **mediation** and **arbitration** providers and hand over the facts necessary to decide the case. Combined with **escrow** and **bonding** services, enforcement becomes feasible without having to rely on aggressive law enforcement in commercial settings. Furthermore strong pseudonyms and reputation systems can provide means to reduce future risk of questionable actors and serve as a social restraint against repeat violations.

Trading posts that provide anonymous deposit boxes that are accessible through tradable digital warehouse bonds are one solution to protect both buyers and sellers by reducing the need to conduct trades in person.

Another idea is the use of "trading tables" that can be reached from both sides only by hard to observe corridors and that feature a barrier between the parties that can not be easily climbed over and which conceal the identity of both parties. Buyer and seller hold each other with one hand during the trade, preventing one side from running away with only one half of the transaction having taken place, and use the other hand to move goods between them. Essentially these trading tables resemble a bank counter except in protecting both sides equally.

Both these services could be provided by competing business clubs or trading halls that differ not only in price, but also by the methods they provide for secure trade.

Another institution provided by the state system that must be replaced by Second Realm shared services is money, and its transfer and settlement. Money is an incredibly powerful cultural symbol that offers ways for mutual recognition and can represent the core values of a society.

It is likely that the Second Realm will focus on independent currencies, probably weights of gold or silver, and should do so to separate itself from the First Realm. Furthermore anonymous digital money and transaction systems can overcome geographical limitations and First Realm regulation and control.

Converting First Realm into Second Realm money, and bridging the gap between physical and digital moneys is a task that makes a special kind of entrepreneur necessary: The Over-The- Counter Exchanger. An OTC Exchanger will buy and sell one currency for another, with the transaction being immediately settled for the customer.

While this business comes with some definite risk, it is also accessible to people with limited capital or reputation, since no paper-trail is created and the settlement risks are minimal. Networks of OTC Exchangers connected with digital currency allow global, almost immediate transfers of value at minimal cost with low risk for the customer, making the Second Realm virtually independent from state controlled banking and money.

Security Through Financial Penalties

As a closing remark on this chapter it is important to recall that financial penalties alone are not sufficient to provide security in trade.

The state is an opponent with deep pockets that can outbid us and wage a war of resources against escrow and bonding systems.

It is therefore necessary to also create a social system that keeps this threat in mind and puts leverage into our hands, lest we want to be outspent.

Chapter 12: The Second Realm – Philosophy

So far this text has dealt with rather depressing subjects like security, defense, analysis of our situation, and the threat of oppression we face. In this chapter the focus will be on the fundamental Why's, the motivation for choosing this struggle, and what it promises us. Why all this trouble? Are we not free already? Do we not enjoy a high level of prosperity? Why bother? Because we are not nearly as free as we should be; as we are maybe meant to be. And what is that Liberty we talk about?

What is Liberty?

Without going too deep into the philosophies of liberty here, one has to differentiate between two major lines of "libertarian" thought. The one is the argument from the consequence, that increased liberty raises prosperity and that prosperity is the goal to target so that hunger and other perils disappear. While we agree on the preferability of the end, our argument is another: That liberty is preferable in and of itself, that liberty alone is reason enough.

The foundation for liberty is a small but powerful word: **Autonomy**. It comes from the Greek words "autos," meaning "self," and "nomos," meaning "Law." It refers to the ability, right, or wish of something to be governed by its own law. Anarchism is therefore not what the media tells us - the presence of chaos or lawlessness - but instead the presence of law chosen by those that are covered by the law, contrary to a law given by rulers to handle subjects (Anarchy: No Ruler). We will be referring to Autonomy in that sense.

The basic ethical axiom of Liberty is **Individual Autonomy** - that each and every person has the right (that is: "is morally justified") to be the final authority over the law he chooses for himself, and that anything that violates this right is a crime.

It is important to realize that this axiom of individual autonomy implies several things.

First, autonomy only extends to the person asserting this right for himself, it does not imply the right to also govern others. By making a decisions about the rules that govern me, I cannot also make a decision on what rules others are bound to. It is only the "Autos", my self, that falls under that law - no one else.

Second, in asserting this right I also have to grant this right to everyone else. This means that under no circumstance may my actions undermine the autonomy of anyone else.

Third, autonomy deals with rules we choose as governing principles for ourselves, but these rules do not have to be realizable nor can we force anyone else to help us enforce them against ourselves and the universe. Whether we like it or not, the realization of our rules is limited by the laws of nature. While we can decide that gravity does not apply to ourselves, it does not change the applicability of gravity. Also, we cannot force others to make our rules work for us, since that would violate their autonomy. At most we can ask for help - not demand it. Just deciding to be always able to eat what we want cannot bind anyone else to provide us with food, or the universe to become a giant vending machine.

Since the application of individual autonomy has these implied limits, and because multiple autonomous individuals can create conflicting laws, it is necessary to define the boundaries in which autonomy can exist.

This sphere of autonomy is known as "property". It is the physical boundaries in which a person is the sole source of law. It is physical because only physical interaction can limit the autonomy of another physical being. And it is necessary so that individuals have room to decide for themselves and know if their decisions are justified.

Any attempt to deny the concept of physical, individual property is an attack on the concept of individual autonomy. Both are interlinked inseparably in the universe we live in.

This brings us to the second fundamental statement about liberty. Liberty is not pure independence or self-sufficiency. Since most of us are unable to satisfy all wants solely by ourselves, and because our spheres of autonomy border upon those of others, we are required to interact with each other - mate, trade, socialize, etc.

The only possible way to do this while preserving individual autonomy is to interact on a voluntary basis, meaning that everyone interacting must do so by his own will and that the only acceptable interaction is one in which both parties agree fully. Any other interaction amounts to a violation of individual autonomy and must be considered a crime.

From this, it follows that even a temporary delegation of decisions to others and any kind of contract or law we chose for social groups must be **unanimously consensual** by all parties delegating or receiving delegation, and all parties joining a group or forming a group that another joins. Anything not meeting this standard violates individual autonomy. Where no such consent can be achieved, the conflicting parties may only end their interaction and separate.

Individual Autonomy is also reciprocal, as mentioned above. Asserting this right also means that we have to grant this right to others, when we deny it to others we deny it for ourselves.

This leads to three major consequences in social interaction.

First, any violation of autonomy (a crime) can only be met and punished by an equal reduction of autonomy of the offending party and the reasserting of the autonomy of the offended party. Crimes are therefore answered by first making the victim whole, and secondly by applying the same harm to the culprit. This constitutes the basic maxim of justice under individual autonomy and the highest justified punishment in any case. However, it leaves room for the victim to pardon the offender whenever the victim chooses, or to voluntarily agree with him on a different form of restitution.

Second, the only party entitled to restitution is the victim, the only party liable to restitution is the offender - an action that has no victim cannot lead to punishment. Any other kind of justice would be criminal in itself, because it violates the individual autonomy of parties that did not act.

Third, asserting one's autonomy also implies the right to defend against violations thereof under the same principles of justice mentioned above. For that, a crime must be underway, and any defense must be relational to the violation. Shooting someone because he might come to your house and steal someday is clearly not permissible, and killing a person for trespass is not either.

Fourth, even if someone has violated our autonomy or has not asserted his own autonomy, does not imply that this person has no autonomy that must be respected by us. A tax collector does not lose his right to autonomy, and it is not justified to hang him from the nearest tree. Nor does the tax-subsidy stolen from your pocket entitle you to use a service over and above the justified amount which would have been found as restitution.

We shall end our excursion into the philosophy of liberty here. Many more elaborate thoughts have been written by others.

Instead, one should stop for a minute and think about the above. Does it make sense? Does it not also ask us to live that way? Is it not so right that it demands our support?

What is it that liberty really gives us? Surely it is not prosperity that makes liberty so important in the first place, though it is a nice side-benefit.

On the one hand, liberty is the fundament to our humanity. It is that what leads us to self-motivation, self-determination, but it is also what allows us to interact pleasantly with others - **Liberty is Peace**. Not a peace based on threats of mutual annihilation or cowardice, but instead founded on what makes us special as humans.

Liberty is what gives us the room to become more human, to live in accord with our ethical and moral beliefs, to progress, to be in peace with others.

In short, **one cannot be fully human without also being in liberty**.

First Implications

The ethics of Individual Autonomy have consequences for the culture of the Second Realm, and the interactions we have with the First Realm.

We do have to respect the individual autonomy of First Realm persons, and even the decisions they have foolishly delegated to institutions and governments beyond their control. This does not mean that the resulting systems are ethical, but they are the will of many. It is thus not for us to take down those systems but rather to offer ethical alternatives, to open doors into the Second Realm where people can fully embrace their humanity through Liberty.

This is required for several reasons. First, it allows us to keep the moral high ground. While this is not a reason in itself, it justifies our position and shows respect to the individuals "on the other side," reducing emotional opposition against the Second Realm. Second, it is necessary to preserve the ethical integrity of the Second Realm. Michael Gaddy said: "The battlefield of freedom is littered with the bodies of those who believe in compromise." Compromising on our ethical foundations in relation to the First Realm will also taint these foundations within the Second Realm.

This calls us to keep the peace with the First Realm as long as it is up to us, to not intervene in the First Realm, to radically keep the two realms separate. There is no place for standoffs.

This strict separation and the respect for individual autonomy also implies that we do not needlessly violate the laws of the First Realm but instead either confine ourselves fully to the Second Realm or live a double-life: Paying taxes in the First Realm and keeping its laws while we are located there, and ignoring the First Realm whenever we are located in the Second. This also includes to not profit from First Realm redistribution and to pay for the services you consume while there.

While these might be hurtful suggestions to many arch-libertarians, they are not without justification. Such a behavior both protects the autonomy of the Second Realm and it shows respect to the individual autonomy of First Realm inhabitants, even though their autonomy is wasted. In addition, it helps us make a decision to invest into the Second Realm and move there completely, fully withdrawing ourselves from the First Realm. For most of us the move from the First to the Second Realm will be a progressive one - a floating scale of radicalization and involvement. Some will stop short for various reasons, bearing the consequences.

To be able to implement such a progressive withdrawal and strict separation makes the drawing of boundaries between the realms necessary. The clearest of these is that our physical and digital temporary autonomous zones and any interaction between only Second Realm inhabitants belongs to the Second Realm exclusively, with everything else being in the First Realm.

Chapter 13: The Second Realm – Culture

Introduction

It is easy to understand that the development of our own culture of the Second Realm is necessary - but attempts to artificially create culture are not only impossible but also counterproductive.

Culture is a spontaneous order that is shaped by the individuals of a society, reflecting their individual decisions and mentalities.

Nevertheless there are several things that contribute to the formation of culture.

One of the most exciting is the influence of art, music, and literature that springs from a cultural context and feeds back into it. The imagination of artists often becomes the inspiration to many. It will be exciting to see the creativity in this area.

Another influence is that of necessity. Culture encodes and optimizes social interactions which are shaped by the reality that society finds itself in. Specific challenges and threats, but also abundances and blessings of environment flow into and through culture. Compare the longing songs of the desert people with the joyful dances of jungle tribes.

Ethical, moral, and religious values are another point to mention. While they are often only reflections of the culture already in place, they also appear in the function of culture-founding factors. This is especially apparent in cultures that did not evolve over a long time but rather rapidly, like much of the United States of America.

The last major contributing factor of new cultural formation lies in the character of the cultural entrepreneurs. It is their boldness, courage, mental clarity and creativity that sows the first seeds of cultural movements and founds new societies. Those who intend to partake in the formation of the Second Realm culture should do so with confidence and boldness, but also in mutual support and encouragement. Many experiments and failures will be required before any significant progress takes place, and every member will partake in the formation of a new society.

Therefore we must limit ourselves to contribute to the factors of necessity and ethical values in this text, but we cannot refrain to also let our dreams flow into it.

A Picture Drawn

The first defining factor for the culture of the Second Realm is its dual identity that consists both of the opposition to the First Realm as well as the embrace, even celebration, of Liberty and its values.

While we are on the one hand outlaws, we are not lowlifes. We are cheerful, colorful but also serious and realistic outlaws.

Our society is not homogenous, hierarchies are close to non-existent. Where hierarchies exist they are through authority of knowledge, action, character and exist only so long as they are actively supported by those affected, which is usually not very long.

Instead, voluntary associations that differ in style and behavior are affiliated in a network of mutual bonds, vouches, and personal reputations. No one leads, but many inspire. It is a dynamic, close, parallel society, sometimes hidden - a crypto society - but always a society of cheerful outlaws who value mutual respect.

Reputation and respect are probably the strongest unifying aspects. While respect is willfully extended until proven misplaced, reputation must be earned by ethical behavior and entrepreneurship. We praise those of us that are successful, those that take risk, and those that pick themselves up after failures. Honesty and contract are holy, and secrets are respected as they not only protect but also add spice to life.

Neither reputation nor respect are empty words for us. They are also ways of binding and help to mutually develop. We communicate them tangibly, by vouching for others, underwriting, and extending bonds to protect our business-partners and peers. In this web of tangible relations, people draw each other up the ladder of affluence, but also quickly sort out evil-doers and scam artists.

We also respect property without becoming slaves to our hosts. Everyone makes it crystal-clear where his borders are, and permission to enter is asked and local rule respected. Many use commonly understood symbols to quickly communicate what they are unable to tolerate on their property.

However, no one has to ask for permission beyond that, or to do anything with what he owns. No one has to be consulted nor licenses procured. Individuals operate for themselves, decentralized, spontaneous - it is easier to ask for forgiveness for honest mistakes than to ask for permission. But we are not without respected order and accepted rules. Criminals have to face the trial of their networks, and hardened thieves usually wake up with their just restitution returned to their victims.

Those that come to destroy our society are not met with torches, but instead are widely shunned and ostracized, not infrequently finding their mugshots at the entry to our zones, some with not-so-friendly notes attached.

Respect for property not only extends to the physical territories we occupy; it is integral to the less visible parts of our world, much of which remains unseen to observers, hidden behind encrypted, anonymous digital communication. This connects us and creates another realm where property is privacy.

We protect our secrets, we value them. Protecting our privacy becomes second nature to us, liberating us from the prying eyes of our enemies. But our privacy is also a key symbol for the autonomy we live. We are taking back what a totalitarian outer world wants to steal from us. What fences are to atoms, data privacy technology is to bits and bytes. We claim that both are owned by us alone: This is our place.

Our places of trade arouse amazement in visitors. As a culture in exile we have developed unusual practices of trade, with some of us excellent in tradecraft. Be it wearing masks when settling a deal or blind handshakes to agree on prices, it only covers half of what is going on. Most trades happen in cypherspace, supported by bonds and reputations extending from the merchant's bar where we meet face to face, to the depths of secure digital escrow platforms.

Overhearing the conversations in one of our clubs irritates the neophyte. Words and customs that are unknown in the filth of the First Realm, and an occasional dispute spiced with curse words like "statist", "Staazi" or "parasite." Nevertheless the newcomer will be welcomed and taught, and given opportunity to prove himself - should he show willingness and skill.

However, not all of us live here all the time. Many lead a double life with only an occasional visit to our markets where they are greeted with their pseudonyms. Others operate their business half a day in the First Realm, and open shop in the Second after sunset. Still others are true ghosts to the First Realm, having no footprint there except for traveling through it from one autonomous zone to another, some of them having perfected their livelihoods in our world, but others that just cannot stand the shallowness of the other side anymore.

We are tribes of mind and soul, not defined by nation or race but by thought and substance. We are everywhere - and we are here to stay.

If you expected a manual of secret handshakes, of words to use and fashion to wear, music to listen to, and opinions that are required - you will be disappointed now.

It is not only our job to create this culture and neatly package it for you. It is your job, and ours, to live it.

Chapter 14: Closing Remarks

The development of mind-tribes, the Second Realm and the increasing decentralization of society is inevitable, should humanity progress further or even survive.

We can see this in a multitude of areas, especially in globalization of trade, the failure of big media, individual digital communication, and the demise of nationalism. Today people often feel nearer to others who live on the other side of the globe and subscribe to similar ideas and culture, than their physical neighbors.

However, this natural process of self-liberation is met by opposition because it also breaks a lot of business models, threatens parasitism, and the mental control over others that many people find so satisfying. It also destroys the status quo and the comfort of everyone relying on it, and it ends the "equal pain for everybody" meme that drives so many who are hurt and abused.

While these might be big words, they are nevertheless true: If we do not act and implement more liberty, the days of humanity might well be numbered.

We live in interesting times that will shape the future, and it is up to us to shape it in a human, a free, and an ethical way. No one else will, and it is time to stop asking for permission or looking for excuses.

If you ever wanted to save the world - this is your chance. And if you just want to live "rightly" yourself and you are not interesting in the big scheme of things, this is for you as well.

And did we mention that it will be fun?

Chapter 15: Next Steps

Should you find this strategy attractive, the question of where to go from here needs to be answered. These are some hints on how to proceed:

1. Make it your goal to achieve liberty based on this strategy or a variation of it.
2. Tell others that you are committed to being active for liberty.
3. Dedicate some of your time on a regular basis to spend working on the Second Realm.
4. Start saving, so you can invest into the Second Realm when opportunities come up.
5. Take digital privacy seriously. Start using PGP, I2P, and similar. Learn about secure behavior.
6. There are some digital autonomous zones out there. Join them and spend time building your reputation.
7. Network with others, but not only in the digital but also in the physical. Have a few drinks together, or start a project. Declare your meetings as being autonomous.
8. Give up collectivist thought, especially asking for permission and requiring others to support you before you do anything.
9. Give up the quest for philosophical homogeneity. We will always differ in the details.
10. Start or support local OTC-Exchangers. Build a position of digital currencies so you can partake in covert commerce.
11. Live a culture of Liberty. Support the autonomy of others visibly: Respect!
12. Insert kindness and strength into the world. Charity and justice are for YOU to do.
13. Encourage others that work for liberty, who invest and produce.
14. If you are an artist, writer, musician, fashion designer (or whatever), run wild in creating our new culture.
15. Begin with defining your boundaries: Shun people who actively attack liberty and deny autonomy to others.

References

1. Mnemonic: Can kings deny decadent dabbler's rules?

2. The digital realm which is heavily protected by cryptography and uses cryptography to model and enforce certain rules.

3. Mnemonic: DO U CAP? (do you cap?)

4. This place is still in operation as this book is written.

BONUS: Next Steps (Redux)
By: Shane Radliff and Kyle Rearden

The following is a redux version of the "Next Steps" portion of Smuggler and XYZ's book, *Second Realm: Book on Strategy*. Overall, the book is fantastic but we both felt this section was severely lacking in quality. Some of these recommendations were redundant, many were badly worded, a couple were later on in the list when they should be towards the beginning, and a few were vague/unclear.

It is our goal to update and improve upon their framework in hopes of giving individuals interested in building Second Realms clear, concise actions they can take to bring their goals into fruition.

1. Make it your goal to live a culture of liberty; spend your free time building the Second Realm, as well as visibly supporting the autonomy of others, whether that takes the form of mutual aid or vigilantism.

2. Give up collectivist thought, especially asking for permission and requiring others to support you before you do anything; also give up the quest for philosophical homogeneity. We will always differ in the details (what's important is the end goal and respect for autonomy).

3. Practice good security culture in both the digital and physical realms. In the former, start using PGP, I2P, ZRTP, OTR, crypto-currencies, etc.; for the latter, practice being the grey man, driving an inconspicuous vehicle, hardening your vonu home, etc.

4. There are some physical and digital autonomous zones out there right now. Join them and help to develop their capabilities. If you don't know of any to join, network with others and form your own; keep in mind, however, whatever reputation you create for yourself is what you'll be judged by.

5. Start saving, so you can invest into the Second Realm when opportunities come up. Encourage others to invest and produce within the Second Realm by patronizing their businesses.

6. Build a position of digital currencies so you can partake in covert commerce (i.e. agorism).

7. If you are an artist, writer, musician, fashion designer (or whatever), run wild in creating our new culture.

8. Begin with defining your boundaries. Shun people who actively attack liberty and deny autonomy to others.

9. Assist your friendly neighborhood proxy merchants whenever possible, as they are your secure gateway to the First Realm.

10. Support your local avenging angels; worst case scenario, if a temporary autonomous zone was breached by the bludg (police), then the angels would have to be activated in order to recondition the State to refrain from disrupting our peaceful zones.

Parting Thoughts:

This is not an exhaustive list for how to start building the Second Realm. It is merely a beginning point. Develop your own methods in accordance with the philosophical intent of the Second Realm and work with others to facilitate efficacious methods of trade outside the First Realm.

More Information

If you'd like to learn more about this topic, please check out the **Building The Second Realm** series we did on **Liberty Under Attack Radio**. It includes 16 episodes, wherein we dive deeply into most every facet of the Second Realm.

Also check out the fiction books, **#agora** and **A Lodging of Wayfaring Men**.

WWW.TINYURL.COM/AGORAANARCHY

Support Us

If you enjoyed the book and found it valuable, please consider making a one-time digital currency donation or become a patron on Patreon for exclusive content!

Bitcoin: 15Bdzduwt92jYFGFaK2NSkPYFTaLbtonJg

Looking for a liberty-oriented publisher?
We can help!

- Proofreading/Editing
- Kindle/Paperback Formatting
- Audiobook Production/Narration
- Marketing/Promotion
- Illustrations/Graphic Design

LIBERTY UNDER ATTACK PUBLICATIONS

WWW.LIBERTYUNDERATTACK.COM/PUBLISH

CPSIA information can be obtained
at www.ICGtesting.com
Printed in the USA
LVHW092255110721
692441LV00003B/186